Song of Myself
and
Other Poems

by Frederick Bauman

Song of Myself
and
Other Poems

CODHILL

CODHILL

Codhill Press
1 Arden Lane New Paltz, NY 12561

A Codhill Book
Codhill Press Books
are published for David Applebaum
first edition
Copyright © 2011 by Frederick Bauman

Song of Myself and Other Poems
ISBN: 1-930337-61-2

Design and Production by Tribeca Imaging
21 Harrison Street
New York, NY 10013
luismorales@tribecaimaging.com

Cover Art by William Tapley:
Art of Color: 16.1
For a further study of color interactions, visit:
tapleycolor.com

Printed in the United States of America

Table of Contents

Song of Myself

I make a pact with you, Walt Whitman –
. . . .
It was you that broke the new wood,
Now is a time for carving.
We have one sap and one root –
Let there be commerce between us.
— Ezra Pound

Part I

Can I celebrate myself or sing myself?

As a formless unknown within this body
As an urge to sing an unformed song
Arising phoenix-like from solar plexus
To appear within me unsung unheard?

Can I perceive this unheard unseen
Barely felt manifestation of myself?

Where does the attentiveness come from
That can perceive a new growth within this body
As something that wishes to be called I
Emerges faintly encompassing
What once was what was called myself
But is now a housing for this new self
Burgeoning expanding outward – delving
Inward lighter than thought awaiting

A gathering of pretenders to the self
Slowly aligning into a ruleable embodiment
Of some force slowly descending within
Spinal column then floating upward
Lightening the crown of this head –

And is it not simply a question of
Remembering, breath by breath, that I exist
And that my place of existence is
Within this newly enlivened body –
Who is this being being witnessed?
Who is this witness perceiving all at once?
Are we all not just what I call myself?

IIVIIVIIIVVII

Suppose I try to see these turning thoughts
And emotions not as myself at all.

Suppose I am what perceives emotions
Thoughts and the sensations of living in
This body seeking to release itself,
Shaking off tensions toward realizing
That I am, perhaps, just experience,
Just movement within silent unknown –
Just urges fulfilled or frustrated
Blossoming blooming disappearing.

Reappearing now as if born into
New worlds emerging through perception
Of myself meeting with fresh impressions
Coming from Sun illumined sprouting
Of multifarious life forms teeming:

Butterflies alighting on rhododendrons,
Barn swallows harvesting unseen bugs,
Deer ranging over lawn cropping dandelions
And you, always with me, each breath renewing
This silent calling settling into
Our bodies inviting us to be erect
And alert to our own movements through space.

Boots, wet from morning dew, tramping along.

As birds herald sunrise a garter snake
Swallows a baby field mouse whose cries
Alert us to another dimension of
What it means to be alive here on Earth.

IIVIIIVVIIIIV

But feeling only partially alive
Myself, I begin to wonder, ponder
What is yet to come alive within this
Collection of bones and flesh and feelings?

Why it is that certain inner movements
Pulse in and out of existence

Like breath tarrying briefly in lungs
Then expanding almost unnoticed through
Noticed aspects of this somewhat aligned
Human body pleading for relaxation
To its missing god withdrawn from this scene
Yet soon appearing in slow parachute
From skull crown down body's sensations –
Glowing solar plexus connecting all.

Had you thought it could be this simple?
To have achieved this new beginning
Without effort with only observation
Uniting us bringing us to this
Starting point just inside of where we are.

When at your ease you observe a spear of
Summer grass knowing its place along side you,
Knowing the urge that brought it forth from seed,
Brought forth your skeletal structure and mine
Structured for walking about on this land.
Just as this spear points skyward we walk erect
Sensing our place, our boots collecting dew –

Blood pulsing quietly through our veins.

IVIIVIIIVVIII

How to begin from here, from pulses
Accepting inability to control
My own experience of who I am –
Yielding to seeing prevarications
Devouring any left over silent urges

To transcend what cannot be transcended,
What must be endured as myself enduring
Myself, as me enduring even you
Forced to confront myself in you
As you struggle not to confront yourself
In me or even in yourself, becoming
Indignant at such a suggestion.

But we can be sensing now silently,

Listening to each other silently,
Questioning assumptions, appearances
The hollowness of our words silently
Forming from whirling thoughts divorced from

This quiet exchange of substances
Which quieten the emotional mind.

So are we now able to share pulsing
Deepening experiencing of these
Inexplicable ascending/descending
Forces absorbed by even subtler
Attentiveness becoming what never
Can be seen or heard but what is presence
Uniting our fractured selves in quiet
Brief experiencing of becoming.

VVIIIIVIIVIII

So this movement toward becoming myself
(And you yourself) beginning with aligning
My scattered body thoughts emotions
Through simple perception by this seeing
Organism which is not thought, desire
Or reaction but silent encompassing
Of all that is housed within this body.

To begin with I am this – all of this,

No static experience but changing
Continuously as energies and
Forces transform each other within this
Skin deepening my experience of myself

Simultaneously letting go of
What I've always taken to be myself.

As cosmoses breath themselves in and out
Of existence, sensations and feelings
Appear as questions materializing
In solar plexus or descending from
Back brain down spinal column lighten
This experience of letting go of
Myself yielding to a sense of presence,
A sense that all is in this deepening

Sense of I am through this questioning of
Who I am – free from attachment to
What I perceive as myself breathing in
And out releasing deeper perceptions
Of this experience of myself.

VIIIIVIIVIIIV

Across what distances our essences
Touch – we feel in each other's renewal
Of what brings us together as living
Embodiment of sacred influences
Expressing themselves physically as what
Draws us together in embraces in
Desire driven culmination of
Our purposes for being here on Earth.

Now we pause admiring each other
Feeling almost breathless, glistening in
Sunlight, receiving rays descending to
Meet our joint aspiration toward our
Renewal our mutual infusion –

As if bees alighting on flowers
Bring us delicate gifts almost weightless
Renewing desireless need for our
Working toward each other's mute perfection
Lightening each other enabling
Each other's sensed intuited return

To the place of ultimate rebirth

Where, poised briefly, we dissolve our concerns
Our lightly given attachments to
Human clutching need deflecting fear
Of being what all along we have been.

And what now lifts away from us lightly
Leaving what has always been here: ourselves.

VIIIVVIIIIVII

Part II

Have you thought nature more beautiful than you?

Have you admired trees coming back to life
Thrusting out new leaves unfurling in air
Have you admired snake's shedded skin's
Delicate expression of growing life?

Yet we're locked within trivial habits
Witnessing sunrise desiring sleep,

Sharing this singular song, this moment:
Brief expanding experience of love
Smashing into selfish habits shrinking
Ourselves into stiff definitions –
Unarticulated but crushing
Effulgent inner blossoming into
Mere admiration of cherry blossoms,
Crocuses, tiger lilies, fireworks.

Finding ourselves drawn into this outer
World of distorted impressions sucking
Out thought, squeezing emotions, tensing body
Dragging us into habitual-
Natural flaying us into slow death

Where – nevertheless- subtle embraces
Descending from just above ourselves
Can take in our stuck-in-habit state
Allowing certain suffering of self,
Certain indications that I am not
My flowering self but this empty sense
Of being an out of control machine.

IIVIIVIIIVVII

How to find what is myself, my being
In this balancing act of urges felt,

In this attentiveness embracing urges
Freeing up new attentiveness, bringing
Our silent embrace, our renewal
Coming alive in emptiness coming
Alive as new being perceived as you
And me rediscovering each other
As I become more myself and you
Are beauty blossoming for the first time.

As you become more yourself and I
See your manifestations as wondrous
Apex of lifelong struggles toward our aim
This fervent moment facing each other
Accepting to be just this perfection
Acting through us toward its culmination.

Behind Nature's terrifying disguise
(Beauty) is this simple cycle of birth
And destruction rewarding us with
Presence – what beauty betrays in its
Rush for appreciation for being
Admired rather than being known.

Lifting away these veils of beauty,

I rediscover you discovering
My emergent self as we work toward
This discovery of two beings as
Forces uniting all that is.

IIVIIIVVIIIIV

Oxen pulling plow through ancient earth
Machines drawing steel through manufactured soil
Christ descending into Hell to retrieve
Our fathers our mothers our patriarchs

Drawing our suffered past into this present
Preparing new soil for new arisings

From soil polluted by chemicals
Parched by global warming, scathed by acid
Rain, undermined by commodities trades,
Drinking water poisoned by shale oil drilling.
Greed spewing buried oil into Gulf of Mexico,
Species vanishing before we discover
Their purpose for existing here on Earth.
What can survive this harrowing descent?

Perhaps just one small particle remains
Uncorrupted – perhaps this tiny center
Of myself somehow touching the same in
You can receive new life from what's above
Expanding our center into new birth.

Have you thought that Earthly life is hopeless?
Have you despaired over poisons in food
Cancers from power grids, chemical plants
Can all of this overwhelm our weak selves
Is there still this single spark that can
Blossom under caring embrace from what
Descends into us from lighter realms above?

I am on the verge of knowing myself

IVIIVIIIVVIII

10

Toward becoming more than worms drowning in
Thunderstorm saturating parched top soil
As humans force mass extinction of fellow
Creatures, humans with each generation
Sink down to fulfill their empty places

Nature fostering more and more humans
Unable to supplant selfish struggles
So deranged by self-imagining
That self-destruction is taken for a
Victory over the need to be
Responsible for our brief existence
For what was once called the gift of life

How to help tattooed dreamers lost from

Themselves valuing trivial pleasures
As awesome experience of themselves?
Valuing fantasies of being cool
Divorced from what makes them human beings.

Entrapped in ghetto forged competition
Weakened by gameboys, circle jerks

Pubescent dreamers gang banging neighbors
Date raping girls so insecure they cling
To the useless schmuck they call their boyfriend
How low must we descend to find the way
Back upward toward what was called, as starting
Point, lower depths of human existence.
For the struggle to fulfill human life's
Yearning for arising toward destiny

VVIIIIVIIVIII

Aglow with quiet radiance as an
Experience of myself now reborn
As a kind of nothingness arising
Evaporating leaving questioning
Just this state of questioning not knowing
Who I am or why I'm here is more
Valuable than mega millions winnings.

And so we can survive this unknowing

What can help to meet our present state
When some sort of awareness descends
From some desirless perspective
Sinking into skin, flesh bones, feelings

Am I this confluence of light and dark
Am I this continuous presence

Can I inhabit foolish teen's grasping
For some definition of his desire
Distorted by peer pressure compels him
To do what absent conscience would forbid
So without condemning this poor lost kid
Just bare his course indifference to Mother
Nature's desperate attempts to return
Us to existence aligned from above

While despairing over lost grandchild
I experience forgiving presence
Descending through me alighting within
Inhabiting breath enlivening skin
Setting solar plexus aglow with light

VIIIIVIIVIIIV

Huge anvil cloud rising thousands of feet
Flashing lightning rumbling thunder
Casting down sheets of rain spitting down hail
Dogs whining children crying thunderclaps
Causing shudders down each being's spine
Awesome expression of Nature's power
Quickly moving on as dogs return to
Sniffing asses and humans to complaints

Returning to our daily cycles leading
Inexorably toward our day of death
To which we are blinded by Nature's need
To keep us tame, obedient until
She harvests us as she feels the need

What effort can be made toward survival
Can a finer replica of myself
Be born within this death bound flesh and bone
Through which breath can whisper Who am I?
Bringing awareness to breath's cavern to
My emerging center in solar plexus
Whence some presence spreads fog-like through me

Dissolving as fog dissolves into this:

A kind of seraphic state exalted
Yet firmly settled into this body
As worlds are meeting in this body
One brief moment of joy alive within

What states available to enter now?
What attentiveness available now?

VIIIVVIIIIVII

Part III

We exist in rarified atmosphere

Having survived Earth bound existence
Looking round wondering if this is
Purgatory – this chest bound struggle
This inability not to see myself

As if clouds floating by above us now
Were pieces of ourselves stretching, pulling

Opening some unknown sensation
Blossoming and wilting in three seconds
As a new cloud drifts through our physical
Selves renewing inner experience
Igniting wondrous presentation
Inviting us to let go of ourselves:
Our knowledge and understanding of what
It takes to rise above complaisancy

To this place which seems to inhabit us
Inviting yielding letting go of me
I see you as if we are both released
From preprogrammed actions/reactions
From the illusion of identity

How to find words both soft and crisp, lighter
Than breath penetrated by powers both
Invisible and silent yet felt as
Questioning dissolving uncertainty
Simply residing within as if
This unknown were all that can be known
As if you and I share this way forward

IIVIIVIIIVVIII

We – in fact – share this way inward finding
Greater and greater silence dispelling

Popcorn cotton candy pizza sushi
Headaches anger sharp dissatisfaction
Because I simply cannot bare to be
An undefined existence moving through
Unknowing toward what appears to be
A fearful sacredness arising each
Moment defenses relax a little
And I am wholly unknown to myself

Why is this state so new why do I gasp
At this realization: I cannot
Know even you – most precious connection
To what I have always known to be life
Letting go of you letting go of myself

What arrives? A godless universe?
An emptiness pervading flesh and flowers
Dirt and its inhabitants – even snake
In rippling movement through grass under
Plywood across lakes and rivers reaching
Through time to an exact replica –
Meditative silence of just this now

Just this rhythm of what takes place within

From here what is there to say or believe
Is there a self? Does existence exist?
Are you and I still able to unite?
In what manifestation of being?

IIVIIIVVIIIIV

It is said that two black holes courting each other
Create perceptible ripples in
Space/time itself as if you and I could
Relax enough to witness our union

Absent this untinkered with confluence
We stare at each other's alien self

We retreat into habitual attractions
We explain and lie and charm each other
All along defeating ourselves with
Alien deceptions entrapping us
Into betrayal of central essence
Of the joy I take in you – you in me
Leaving heartache salved with empty pleasures
A crushing descent into my own hell

Where finally we find each other
Shocked into stillness awaiting descent
Of the one substance, vibration or
Attentiveness that can bring the one
Realization that we are nothing

But a manifestation of what called
Us into being brought us together
So that now we are no more or less than
This blossoming simultaneously
Within each of us within the Sun and Stars
Feeding our galaxy's black hole with our
Own essences – bringing renewal

Of this life we always share together

IVIIVIIIVVIII

Now there is this possibility for
New release. What appears firm can slowly
Dissolve. I never realized I was
Clinging to so much. Behind this pen, as
It floats on this paper summoning words

That are now able to lift free of their
Definitions to exude sound and other
Vibrations that inform me that they are
Transient beings just as what I call
Myself can be allowed to float free
Evaporate into space exposing
This raw sense of being doubted by myself

Who breathes what substance into being?

Thieves and warriors struggle on missing this
Nadir of resistance receiving this
Silent cascade of awakening to
A certain downward Christening action

Aiming to stimulate this opening
Of what had appeared to be awareness.

So a continuous sense of dissolving
Leaving no trace behind of its actions
Leaving only awareness of what is
Undissolved: persistent traces of old
Identity awaiting their own chances
For release from this complex arrangement
Clinging to itself as if it were myself
As if these frozen habits had being

VVIIIIVIIVIII

17

Within this ongoing dissolution
There are hints of something new, a birthing
Of what is lighter than perception
Which sees without being seen and hears
Without being heard, thinks without being
Thought of, perceives without being perceived?
What appears within the center of myself?

Am I now this act of welcoming I?

How to be appropriate housing for this
Visitor who begins to settle in
Offering me the possibility
Of serving this unperceived sense of self

Here is wonderment. Here is questioning
Who is the questioner who is questioned?

What can allow a continuous
Visitation what can this complex of
Thought, feeling, sensation, do to arrange
Itself as permanent host and subject
To this superior intelligence,
Superior presence so that it will
Not once again retreat from my own presence
But becomes master of myself?

So far this celebration of myself
Is it premature, one sharp reaction can
Corrupt delicate forging into
Unaware self-centeredness unaware
Destroyer of sacred earthly bounty

VIIIIVIIVIIIV

As new sensations appear within this
Earthly body as a recognition
Arises not allowing any part
To claim credit for this more refined state
That is mine but universal
Yet has not fully laid claim to this voice
Which still holds allegiance to self-image –
A mirror of my disappearing self.

What else exists within this gradually
Emptying mirror? Is that what whispers
Within these words voiced on these pages
Baring witness to an embodiment
Of what is unmanifest in this life

As more of what is felt but unknown
Begins to inhabit this body
Fostering a warm deepening glow
In solar plexus suggesting nascent
Awakening of a deeper self that
Has been hidden guide forcing deep struggles
Exacting payment for this life on Earth

Am I this awakening, am I here?

Am I this lone answer to my question
Of who I am standing in this sphere
Of radiance slowly penetrating
Your awareness of imminence within?

I am, we are – as we disappear and
Re-emerge exactly where we started.

VIIIVVIIIVII

Reconnaissance

And I was thinking why does thought
Go round in circles leading to nothing
But empty dreams and sour perceptions
Encrusting all I know into my death?

●

Wandering down wooded lane leading toward

Some assumed understanding some wistful
Longing for what lurks behind random thoughts
Snaking down spine unperceived memory
Shredded by denial hurkled within

Our physical form embodying some
Emergence of what's sought for down this lane

But what flowers orchid-like drooping down
Yet promising more than what can be felt
By simply allowing what is seen to
Be absorbed as this impression of our
Continually kaleidoscopic
Experiencing – just underneath our
Recognition of what passes for life
Lived in harmony with our illusions

So this lane leads into another one
Promising much with entwined florid vines
Climbing sturdy oaks as if Eden bound
Yet concealing inner hatred as if
Hell beings were clambering up our spines

As florid vines become our constrictors
Expressing resentments, desires to
Crush or strangle our presumed enemies

As we invisibly rage against those
Who seem to stand in our way, but now we
Start to hear faint refrain: I am the way
I am this within all our confusion

•

Whence comes this wretchedness, this misery?
Just willing to be desire driven

Like caterpillars losing track of their
Butterfly fates, losing touch with urges
To enwrap themselves in silken cocoons
Following only craven distractions for
This and that: game boys, iphones, weight watchers
Cigarettes beer-can collections, ghostly
Fantasies of a life without struggle
Perfection achieved through clutching phantoms.

Awakening from dreams of loneliness
Of tiny rodents crawling along spine
Provoking urges to grasp whatever
One fears to lose simply slipping away
All our treasured well displayed tchotchkes.

Possessed by anguished spirits gathering
Within our flesh armored to avoid visions
Of ourselves squirming to avoid seeing
How we clutch delusional images
Of not clutching but offering blossoms
Of love opening within the hearts of
Fellow beings grateful for our presence

Alone within our crowded selves dreaming

Unable to hear inner calm voice's
Resonance offering clear directions
Leading back here for I am the way

To where there's nothing left to grab or clutch

•

But I'm feeling pretty good today just
Relaxing through skin, muscles, bones and gut
Thought yielding to sensations pulsing through
This form inhabited by what I am /

•

Soaring northern harrier challenging
Competitors screeching, proclaiming what
Enables him to claim this human scarred
Quadrant of ancient Earth's lush plantation

Worms devouring their way enriching dirt
While knowing only to keep on going

Red fox trotting succinctly across dark
Lawns scouting out mice, erect alert
Driven by hunger and tradition
To harvest lush rodent population
Acting as if entitled to claim mole
Bodies as well earned booty, as demesne
Yet only hunger driven to achieve
Purposes unknown to flesh craving fox

Multitudinous ladybugs appearing
On windowsills climbing up window glass
Landing in breakfast tea, crawling along
Elbows, chair backs, newspapers being read
By tolerant humans' mock affection

Delighted humans giving pet names to
Ladybugs landing on orange juice glass
Interpreting harriers screeching cry
Attributing cleverness to fox's

Dignified trotting across country road
Digging up night crawlers for fishhook fate
Presuming to command our place in life

Camouflaging whispers: I am the way

•

Mostly unperceived haunting emptiness
Constantly crammed with thoughts, TV, email,
Exercise machines, spider solitaire,
Three new pairs of shoes, vitamin water,
Ebay's hidden treasures munching nachos

Just got to have Coca Cola Snickers
After twenty minutes on stair master
Munching chip and dip sipping soda while
Watching bodies pulled from earthquake wreckage
Just got to have that alpaca sweater
Just one more Michelob / pistachios
By the handful I just can't help myself

Even after sexually sated

Incessant advertisements' sex allure
Spurring craving for unneeded garments
Hair color beach vacations cigarettes
Hot one who shares morning elevator

At night we dream of filling up our void:
New patio ensemble imagined

Now waking to a realization
That breaks down all craven fantasies for
What can build up moat, drawbridge and castle
Mimicking immunization from our
Gnawing fears of being left alone with
Ourselves in vermin infested image

That stands behind our flattened mirrored selves
But then to realize: I am the way.

•

Toward some sort of awakening within
Solar plexus and spreading, lightening
Some body within body's sensations
As if being were blossoming within.

•

What makes those gods think they're better than us?
Their reserved parking on Mount Olympus
Metamorphosing into mere humans
And meddling in their petty affairs
Posing for sculptures and paintings as
If mere bric-a-brac could immortalize
Their vein striving for mortal dominance

Humans: text messaging their nothingness

Snakes' slithering explorations of
Grasses, brush harvesting rodent excess
What entitles rattler to proclaim its
Reign over human plowed planted terrain

And what gives anguished spirits a right to
The edges of perception stealing breath

And then those hated beings deserving
Their own hatred. We knew them once in life
Crushing childish urges to burgeon
Into real beings able to lift
Human spirits above mere godliness
Toward exhumation of all that was lost
In sinking selfish dreams of triumphant
Desecration of what we know to be

Forgotten memory of what we once
Knew to be ourselves conveying ancient
Knowledge no longer comprehensible
Except one feint echo: I am the way
Toward what was once called self-recognition

•

Long past twilight defying extinction
No longer visible on Olympus
Haunting language and imagination
Yet not perceived commanding thunderbolts
Urging heroes into bloody battles
Erupting through volcano's frozen crust
Guiding or destroying every ship at sea
Embodying themselves in sun, stars, moon

Elevating themselves above human
Strivings deigning to meddle in human
Conflicts inspiring to aspire
To be godlike ourselves then crushing our
Emulations of their condescension.

What is there beyond proud accomplishment
Beyond gods – is there God or just some void?
Powers descending from Olympus and
Spreading across earth expressing passion
For forcing humans into lookin' good!
Making these higher beings proud of their
Weaker desire addicted charges

Convinced that here we can do no better

Gods leading us via thoughts and desires
Via our secret worshipping forces
Unacknowledged in our constant dreaming
In our inner disjointed consciousness:

A subtle subconscious voice proclaiming
I am the way — toward what awakening?

•

So what cannot be explained can be felt
And this experience we share right now.

Compass

Munching clover, cottontail rabbit
Eyes, constantly alert, spy hawk
Circling, continually alert for prey.

Young rabbit quickly hops toward protection of
Ancient crab apple tree whose canopy
Shields him from hawk's focused attention.

Wish for perpetual life spurring hawk
Rabbit and apple tree in their assigned
Forms of natural urges evolving.

Spying spent dandelions at tree's base
Rabbit clips off at ground level
Chews them in like child sucking spaghetti.

Energized briefly rabbit begins his
Licking grooming ritual keeping off
Forces attracting him toward inertia –

To be always ready to be what we
Have no choice but to be – just rabbit,
Just apple tree, just garter snake, just me.

Leaving off grooming rabbit discovers
Clover flowers all around him giving up
Pollen to bees in symbiosis.

Now rabbit's turn devouring flowers
Plant and animal fulfilling functions
In unperceived exchange of substances.

I – pervading soil, plants, animals –
At my ease with vibrant play of
All forces/forms constituting life.

•

Moving out from under wind blown roofing
Shingle, garter snake, calm alert, driven to
Duty by hunger launched inquiry.

Spying almost invisible movement
Through grass, hawk dives toward prey, but garter snake
Slithers quickly to apple tree protection.

Wish for continuous existence
Ensampled in snake's inborn quickness
As hawk retreats to nearest lookout post.

Yeah, hawk has hopes, but patience and stillness
Of snake and rabbit prevent perception
Of his now disappearing evening meal.

Finally dusk's lost visibility
Frees snake and rabbit for their foraging.
Snake approaches, strikes, devours tree frog.

To be ready to cope with descending
Darkness garter snake senses his way to
Shelter under old roofing shingle.

Eventually rabbit moves back to
His simple nest under neighboring porch –
Beckoning slumber enwrapping rabbit.

Left to itself, crab apple tree relaxes
Receiving condensation's nighttime dew
Resting from photosynthetic duties.

I become convinced, disappearing in darkness,
That one force is at work here balancing
Inner/outer urges in one being.

•

Years without pruning have turned apple tree's
Branches into dense canopy yielding
Lots of leaves, skinny branches, wormy apples.

First sign of light, rabbit is out grazing
Hawk soaring proclaiming dominion over
This former farmstead now summer retreat.

Wishing to further ennoble himself
Hawk soars higher, proclaims louder until
Hunger pulls him downward seeking prey.

As Sun's rays begin to warm grassy soil
Garter snake slithers out from shingle home
Which had absorbed warmth to make him limber

Sensing hawk's presence, snake makes himself
Invisible, blending into grasses
Then darts toward crab apple tree.

To be quiet enough to co-exist
Under silent apple tree's canopy
Three beings unaware of each other

Moved in unison with growing grass,
Breezes rustling leaves, Sun moving cross sky
Knowing why we're here and what we serve.

Syncretism supposed by philosophers
Intelligent design by others
Seeking to avoid fathoming themselves.

I am left confronting my ignorance
Of why rabbits, snakes and trees share this life
This one so well proclaimed by soaring hawk.

•

Snake, appearing bright, alert, confident
Moving, pausing, tongue intuiting search
Passes rabbit without interest or care.

Yielding to silent snake, rabbit remains frozen
Then briefly resumes harvesting clover
Flowers as nonchalantly as he can be

Wishing for becalmment, umbrellaed by crab
Apple tree as if guardian of inner
Connection with every aspect of life.

Fearfulness briefly dissolving so rabbit
Hops parallel to garter snake as they
Pursue apparently separate aims.

Each being self-assured center of the
Universe conducted by whatever
Vibrant force residing within us all –

To be as light as butterfly alighting
On clover flower inches from rabbit's
Nose, fluttering on settling by snake,

Lingering too long as instant strike
Collapses butterfly into belly
Wadding swallowed matter-of-factly.

Moving on snake and rabbit inhabit
Themselves under crab apple's immobile
Equipoise growing, dying all at once.

I find myself silent observer of
Apple tree, rabbit, snake, circling hawk
As if all were residing within me.

•

Each blade of grass slithered through by snake
Each clover plant feeding rabbit's belly:
Transformers of Sun's diurnal blessing.

Light's energy captured by grass released
To cottontail rabbit by digestion
Leaving behind excremental residue.

Wished for cyclic completion as scat is
Dissolved into soil and absorbed by
Grasses once again transforming Sun's rays.

Meanwhile hawk, perched on utility pole
Spots young skunk crossing driveway and launches
Into air quickly swooping down on prey

Skunk's spray no defense against predator
Lacking olfaction. Hawk relishing each
Bit of flesh torn from putrid carcass.

To be unwilling sacrifice, to have
One's life ripped from one in an instant
Each death serving nature's purpose,

Yielding to lightly felt sense of freedom
Garter snake and rabbit gradually
Move out from apple tree's guardianship.

For at least one more day, snake and rabbit
Survive carrying on delusion
Of existing for ourselves alone.

I wonder what perspective
Will open up new vistas of ourselves
As particles of this vaster unknown whole.

●

Lifting up away from us a rigid
Definition of what we encounter.
Each moment of movement through this world

Measured now by a new movement downward
Flowing down spine enlivening muscle
Skin awakening dormant sense of self

Wishing for deeper silence, we let go of
Timelines, desires to manipulate
All around me as adjuncts of myself.

Snake slithers by me having no need to
Acknowledge my existence as rabbit
Keeps his distance from what he does not trust.

Yawp sounded by hawk acknowledges no
Equal, proclaims aggression free from self-
Centered fantasy, free from delusion

To be tested again and again
Having no choice but to express what's in
Him to be expressed – what is needed now;

For what was once called the wheel of fortune
Is simplistic analogy for what
We, invisible particles, are part of

Eying cottontail rabbit, hawk, grass leaves
Sun and clouds unable to acknowledge
What subsumes us in vast sense of being.

I hear my own lack of being in
Pronouncing this word "I" as if I was
Entitled to call myself into being.

•

Finally even careful silent hunter
Fools himself assuming exemption from
Lightning attack snatching him up into

Efficient hawk claws – soon to be pierced
By hawk's sharp ripping beak –
Gruesome discovery of non-existence.

Wished for perpetuation of himself
Denied as hawk finishes ripping him
Apart – nothing left in his place at all.

Left alone rabbit forages without
Awareness of garter snake's absence,
Harvesting clover, looking for mate.

Male turkey roams past pecking up insects
Crab apple tree's almost ripe fruit attract
Several deer who rear up snatching apples.

To be in the midst of celebration
Of this bounty yet so myopic each
Being's vision closed by survival.

Senses closed by urge just to endure –
Unaware of participation in
What has been called forth from this Earth's surface.

Year after year this same memory-less
Enactment of needed exchanges
Of forces manipulating us.

I wonder as I stand by this same crab
Apple tree, what has brought me here today?
And what calls forth this wonderment I feel?

Food Court

Entering mall food court as if landing
On totally synthetic planet, we
Receive cacophonous shocks from undesigned

Manipulations by men climbing up
Career ladders by projecting hollow
Images designed to ignite hunger.

Am I beckoned by chick-fil-a or
Pepperoni pizza, lo mein or burgers –
Fries saturated with engineered oil?

Ordered food served in foam tripartite
Plates like dog food slopped in bowl. Soda
Capped and strawed ready for instant sucking.

Atmosphere of electrical leakage
Penetrates skin, dulls perception
Like invisible insects buzzing round.

Now as we wander in search of empty
Table, a subtle sensation as if
We're all ants swarming over road kill.

Eating dead food supplemented by
Unearthly chemicals not noticing
Body's shocked vibrations absorbing this stuff.

Carrying greasy trays to garbage can,
Sensing slight indigestion, a little lightness
As if moon struck – hunger numbed not satisfied.

•

Benjamin Franklin, as if descended
From another planet enters food court
Hunger driven into sense numbing din,

Ordering ribs and pork fried rice not sure
Whether it's dog or pig he's being served,
Stares at plastic fork and knife balloon sealed.

Am I in the right place? What brought me here?
Why are all these people half naked?
Why do their children whine and cry so much?

Before leaving, he stares at menu
Posted above the cook's work area
Seeing men eating it – may be OK.

Passing trash barrel sees many throwing
Out half their food, uncertainty arising.
Why do all these people seem to be dead?

Now Ben, after this weak conundrum,
Decides he simply needs to satisfy
His belly's incessant craving for food.

Finally seated, feeling somehow like
An insect about to suck human blood
Spreads napkin on lap, unsheathes plastic fork,

Lifts pork fired rice to mouth, tastes something strange
While hunger driven swallow prevents his
Spitting out what's clearly not human food.

I see him sitting next to me haunted
By his puzzlement, wondering why he's
Been condemned to visit his former world.

•

Jefferson, studying menu, wishes
His man was here to serve him, intrigued by
Italian names like pizza, calzone,

Realizes the moon shaped flat bread is
Pizza, orders it with pepperoni,
Ponders trash barrel, looking for a seat.

Am I here to discover what's become
Of my godchild, democracy? Seems
To be where people at large gather.

Seats himself near light skinned black family
Who remind him of his own children,
Studies them brushing flies from their pizza.

Taking his first bite he's puzzled by the
Earthy bouquet of flavors intruded
By grease from curious sausage.

Now looking around – there's no order here.
Artificial light makes him wish he were
Horseback riding instead of with these people.

Watches whole streams of families entering
Is this the same planet where he once resided?
- Longing for his Virginia plantation.

Watching dark skinned blacks ordering their food
Feels urge to send them to slave quarters
With dogs and fleas as sleeping companions.

"I am mightily dismayed," wondering
"Am I ready for democracy?
Are there any men among these sheep?"

●

Abraham Lincoln pausing solemnly
Wondering if dog meat is in what is
Called Mexican food. "Chimichanga, please."

Having second thoughts, studying menu
What is the difference between burritos,
Taccos and so on? Is this food for men?

Feeling out of place in his ill-fitting
Black suit, Abe wonders, "What am I here for?"
Not finding answers, he picks up tray.

Abe always feeling haunted by fate
As if full moon lurking over shoulder
Trashing all his dreams of a better life.

Feeling like giant awkward insect
Abe seats himself, removes his hat, saddened
By brash insecurity around him.

"Now," he thinks, "have I come back to free
These slaves?" Looking around at everyone
Blind to what draws them into such chaos?

So removed from Earth they grew up
Eating factory make food, Abe can see
None had ever split logs or raised food.

Awareness of themselves as remote as
Planets winking from above at night their
Presence blocked out by street and neon lights.

Has anyone been emancipated
Since I signed a decree I hoped would end
Even this invisible oppression?

●

Teddy Roosevelt, seated at table,
Waiting to be served, flies buzzing round him.
Mall cop: "Can't sit there without buying food."

Ends up eating teriyaki beef
In honor of the Mikado and modern
Japanese nation emerging on Earth's backside.

Am I ready to take charge in this place?
"Bully for the Nips, not bad this stuff.
I'll explore this crepuscular scene."

Entering once again this entrance
Teddy senses planets influence here –
Some sort of stagnant endless revolving.

Where are my hunting dogs? Ordering up
Some chicken teriyaki slopped into
Foam and bagged he looks to return homeward.

Now, as if a new sign within his
Chest arrests him, he has no hounds, no
Authority here – only a witness lost.

Just a man studying men, he
Does not understand like a blind tarot
Reader looking for some understanding.

Dumping much of his repast in trash bin
Looking round once more. What happened to
My efforts to make men of weaklings?

As I watch him slowly dissolve in my
Imagination, I wonder what brought
About unrecognized desolation.

•

FDR, eyes twinkling through pince-nez,
Gobbling hot dogs with calm dignity,
Sensing his connection with the People.

Planetary alignment that brought him
To the Presidency summoned him to
Enter this food court in search of ourselves.

Am I among the People, are these sad
Preening people the result of my
Shepparding their grandparents out of hell?

He's remembering dachshund shape ordering
Hot dog from dreamy uniformed child
Serving them up across Nathan's counter.

Seeing one man among these teen children
He watches as this man ascends ladder
To change daily special on the menu.

Now caught between brilliant familiar past
And apparent chaotic present, he
Asks himself how to understand what's here.

Watching as moon sinks into trash barrel.
Franklin D. Roosevelt feels let down by what
Transpires in front of him: dying world –

Men in tank tops, women in short shorts
Children sucking plastic tits, fighting,
Wholly lost from contact with their parents.

"I can't remember why I became
President. There seems to be no awareness
Of being lost or way of being found."

•

As waxing crescent moon ascends over
Food court, Martin Luther King, Jr.
Eyes over flowing trash can with distain.

Flies buzzing round trash seem to follow him
As he finds his seat in quadrant where
Only white people are eating their lunch.

Am I in the right place? What message
Can I bring to these self-satisfied
Dreamers solipsising in their playland?

Eating something called chick-fil-a, finding
Not enough taste or life to recognize
Whether this originated on Earth

Or some planet one occasionally
Glimpses entering or leaving food court,
Drooping in evening sky as if pleading.

Now looking around once again, he suspects
That his life's efforts toward liberation
Lead only to this somnambulism.

What does it mean for his people to have
Equal status with pre-programed white
People who are no more free than dogs?

Is there a man in this house, is there a
Living being who can order living
Food from consciously compiled menu?

"Have I left all this behind and become
Living spirit of struggle to be free
Enough to arise toward my own being?"

Three Jays in Winter

Feeling out of sorts, not quite sure what's wrong
Tight shoulders, tensing gut, thoughts whirling round;
Yet some thought of harmony existing
Unrealized – maybe just unperceived

•

I glance out frosted window spying jay
Lifting off snowy elm branch announcing
Approach to frozen bird bath with screeching
Coded message warning off other jays
Heart beat radiating warmth within down
Blanket covered in blue/grey/white feathers
Sharp fingered feet stretching to grasp ice surface
As jay alights slips falls slides complaining
Scrambling panicked feet grasp wings flutter
Sliding across ice bum bumping into
Stone rim stability not recognized
Slipping again slowly gliding
Toward stone rim now seen as stability
Righting on rim smoothing ruffled feathers

•

Ambling round rim eying frozen surface
Beak shocked pecking ice – stolid puzzlement
Testing surface foot slipping off balance
Righting body circumambulating
Ice on sure footed rim determined to
Penetrate frozen winter resistance
Stepping slowly precisely on surface
Taking two steps feet slipping above head
Wings grasping rim jay quickly rights himself
Now intuiting what balancing act
Can sustain vertical mobility

In silent sojourn across slick surface
Achieving opposite rim jay perches
Silently taking in his situation

•

Body tensed against thought of harmony
Unanticipated fears calling forth
Dark hints of longing for escape from this
Failure to perceive beyond fixed thoughts

•

Then I see second jay approaching
Shouts hawk screech to frighten off settler.
First jay, settled into his body, not
Overawed, squeaks response like rusty pump.
Second jay circles bath screeching as
He calculates how to successfully
Confront fellow jay as bird bath master.
Alights on rim facing his obstacle,
Studies ice surface, studies first jay,
Circles round rim challenging, threatening.
First jay moves to counter challenge head on.
Second jay leaps to position himself
Across frozen bath water facing his
Perceived nemesis's embodiment

•

Wishing he had this bird bath to himself
Yet feeling urges toward brotherhood
Second jay screeches broken melody
Inviting first jay to reveal himself.
First jay ruffles/unruffles his feathers,
Projects his loudest hawk imitation,
Quizzically staring at his visitor,
Insistently settling into his stance.

Second jay angrily repeating his
Own encoded stipulations of his
Terms for receiving members into a
New tentatively conceived brotherhood.
No resolution just two jays staring,
Posturing, screeching mindlessly stubborn

•

This sense of wholeness now felt underneath
Habitually closing of emotions,
Muscles, perceptions cutting off from breathing
Organism opening and closing.

•

I then saw third jay alighting on
Overhanging branch studying his
Fellow beings listening thoughtfully
Hankering for a bit of harmony
Summoning from his lungs and throat and beak
An interceding song, a melody
Of sorts emerging from his whole body,
Resounding through this little patch of Earth.
For one moment two jays below are touched,
Staring above, at each other, silent
Puzzled by inner urges to find this
Haunting call within their own beating heats.
All three jays momentarily silent
As if honoring nascent immergence

•

Can one jay intercede to harmonize
Stubborn squabbles between stubborn strangers
Whose stark squawkings unconsciously invite
Or require intermediation
This third jay, sensing urges in his wings,

Fluttering up, gliding around bird bath,
Somehow body able to precisely
 Alight amid two jays' confrontation.
Feeling new impulse emerging from lungs,
Enunciating warbling squawks at each,
Surprised competitor who then begin
Similar warble-like attempting
And as if awakening to himself
Jay finds himself understanding fellows
Three jays improvising single language

●

Listening supplanting thought inviting
Clear perception of silence within squawks.

Spring Sequence

Simple scientific explanations
Of Earth's axis and rotation round Sun
Leave unaccountable complexities
Interwoven between snowmelt and solstice.

•

Late March thawing in progress – areas
Exposed to sun showing brown dormant grass
Shaded areas still covered in white
Snowpack sheets receding some each day.
All turkeys gathering from snow packed woods
For miles round into community
For just this purpose of perpetuating
Themselves through generating progeny.
Largest mature jakes proclaiming readiness
To implant their essences in females
Receptive and longing to nurture poults
Into adulthood into serving this need
To keep turkey's being ongoing in
This complex of abundant life on Earth

•

Very first day ground is thawed enough for
Worms to be captured, robins appear in
Numbers hopping, listening, pecking up
Worms 'til new snowfall briefly banishes them.
Raptor screech announcing first appearance
Of northern harrier gliding to
Utility pole perch – intense, alert
To rodent movement across dormant lawn.
Each day new bird appearance – wood ducks rest
On roofs on journey farther north – phoebes
Gently announce their assumptions of

Territory for rivals and for mates.
New order now being established as
We begin to understand why we're here.

•

Choreographed appearance of worms
And robins, hawks and rodents, unfurling
Of tree leaves and insect appetites –
Cycles of decimation and abundance.

•

Red maple buds are now blossoming
Tiny red flowers on massive tree – no
Sign of beauty, no hint of ability
To send seed soaring across distances
Yet little flecks of deep red make their way
From ancient tree – outward expression of
Some will to persist in present form and
To expand into future generations
Allowing us to feel silent effort
That is required for us to become
Ourselves – our own expression of needed
Urge to propagate this present moment
Leaving us in continuous motion
Leading all of us forward to right here.

•

New generations having been cast
Abroad, red maple renews itself through
Slow unfurling of buds into leaves
Each day almost unnoticed opening
As insects awaken lodged in bark
Inviting nuthatches serious playful
Upside down foraging in bark crevices
Symbiotic animated expression

Of forces that complete leaf unfurlment
Inviting mocking bird to alight atop
Ancient maple as pileated woodpecker
Harvesting larvae from rotten former limbs.
Vociferous mocking bird announcing
That renewal has been achieved again.

•

Snake sojourning in stacked firewood
Turkeys leading poults on foraging walks;
Canadian goose standing watch as
Flock pecks up insect larvae, defecating.

•

Tiny shoots of new grass appearing through
Old brown remnants of last year's lifeless growth
Interspersed with shoots of dandelion,
Thistle and other uninvited plants.
Pregnant doe just weeks from birthing her fawn
Grazes over vast lawn ripping up new
Grass and old – just glad not to eat sapling
Bark anymore – contented with small shoots.
Lawn finally covered with full green growth
Doe, eating, luxuriating in grazing
As fawn's awkward frolics are interspersed
With nursing mama's milk from the source
Extending backward past grass digestion
To Sun's renewal of our presence here.

•

Turkey leading new poults foraging through
Woods cross lawns pecking up insects, worms, spiders
Exploring every aspect of terrain
Seeking mastery of one's world as hedge
Against unanticipated changes:

Thunderstorms, coyotes, hawk predation.
As summer heat approaches and berries
Slowly ripen, poults molt and mature.
Lawnmower cutting down fast growing spears.
Unmuffled engine noise driving turkeys
Into wood's shelter pecking up tiny
Tree frogs – always finding the nearest way
Leading through genetic history,
Once again arriving at our source.

•

Brief abundance established by solstice:
Coyotes deftly harvesting their crop.

Summer Doldrums

Hanging round swimming pools or swimming holes
Picking shucking sweet corn, ripe blueberries
Ambling barefoot over grass and gravel
Noticing buzzard circling low.

•

Without dark clouds, hail storms, rumbling thunder
Inner darkness grows breeding tensing doubt.
It's a perfect day – Sun, soft drifting clouds
Yet some gnawing urge beckoning us down
As if being dropped out of our habits
As if careers, family, beds and dinners
Dehydrated into non-existence
Leaving us clutching for what is not here.
So in spite of radiant Sun's light and
Warmth, darkness invades mind and emotion
Stiffening muscles tensing gut rusting
Joints as dread steals into daily tasks
Harvesting worm infested apples
As moth larvae devour our sweaters.

•

Swimmer diving from elm branch toward deep
Dark swimming hole's unseen, guessed at bottom;
Rising up before total darkness reached –
Simply defeated by body's buoyancy;
Climbing old elm to higher branch.
Swimmer determined to touch bottom.
One more leaping dive plunging arrow-like
Through dark water hand touching rock bottom;
Casually rising up triumphant;
Pulling himself onto rock shore pride mixed

With dissatisfaction recognizing
Only foolish aim had been achieved.
Drying dressing haunting emptiness
Occupies unacknowledged sense of self.

•

Eagles soaring higher catching thermals.
Blue jays squabbling, Sun slowly crossing sky
As we gobble hot dogs suck up sodas
Dipping chips in guacamole, salsa.

•

Can satiating entrenched desires
Defend us from silence of unknowing,
Dread of being incomplete, vacuous
Left hanging on a cross of conviction,
All our certainties becoming nails
Tearing through flesh holding us imprisoned
While nightmares replace perception we writhe
Struggling to escape terrification.
We are unable to see what we've done,
How we've hammered ourselves in place by
Barbecue pit where we swap jokes with
Neighbors, claim the secret's in the sauce.
All along this secret in me, in you
Clambering within seeking to be borne.

•

What can this involuntary suffering
Lead us to? Can one voluntarily
Open to this experience, to this
Intense need to be here in the midst,
Here where – still joking with neighbors – we can
Also be attuned to excruciating
Loneliness, exquisite struggles to just

Stay with what was being avoided,
What would bring tears or anger if it had
A cause – something to blame but is really
Just the core of one's self radiating
As if we are each a sun within this
Galaxy of human souls wandering
This Earth in search of humanity.

•

Urge to escape life's struggles through summer
Pleasures giving way to unacknowledged
Regrets, subtle sinking into dark moods
Washed away with marguerites and wine.

•

And so we wander among ourselves held
In curious suspense, able only
To recognize fellow strugglers by
This painful resonance pulsing within –
Which becomes an anchor steadying us
Against waves of desire, worry, dreams.
We seem to rise above blind reaction.
Solar plexus keeping us on course
Radiant pain as compass and quadrant
Enabling us to faintly perceive a
Path leading upward toward transformation
Of doubt, worry into experience
Conceiving voyage into this present,
To this meeting place of intense forces.

•

Diver's buoyancy transforming now into
Simple insight that what happens is true,
That this experience of ourselves is
What can lead us up toward understanding.

Entering this realm lurking in our
Bodies eschewing satisfaction,
Baring burning chest-bound sensations.
Tottering between despair and hope
I am now waxing in this burning light
As we feel our way allowing ourselves
To be participated in by this
Experience we've always avoided:
Just staying here listening to you
We begin to arise toward letting go.

•

Sighing at pools edge complaining about
The heat – unsensed need to be more ourselves.

Autumn Awakening

Once more subtle orange and yellow specks
Amidst this forest of green; once more
A slight chill in the air reminds us of
Verdure's retreat as Sun seeps southward,

•

Still craving chimichangas, still craving
Margueritas, crepuscular liaisons
Just out of sight from betrayed partners –
Still craving limitless draining pleasures.
Haunted by gnawing realization
Of summer's end, of losing squandered bounty
As each day leaves give up their life turning
Red, yellow, orange as their death rattle.
Senses retreat giving up their dominance
Allowing a fuller experience
In which desires submit to conscious
Understanding of a need to harmonize;
Sensing we are particles of a
Transitioning whole pricking us alive.

•

Chill air descending from Canada
Forced into retreat by advancing front
Moving up from Gulf of Mexico – yet
Southern air giving up its dominance
As slowly the jockeying of heat and cold
Is being won by new arctic buildup
And we see plant after plant withering;
Dying fields become vast graveyards
Birds in whole flocks migrate, adapt or die –
Deer losing weight, weak and infirm, lost to

Coyote attack as coyotes also
Approach starvation, become more alert
Awakening to this need to be themselves
Inhabiting fur, devouring weakness.

●

Simple signs of death after last night's frost
Windswept stark barebones landscape withdrawing
Into itself preparing for snow/ice
For this land's deathlike hibernation.

●

Frost covering on ground, frost covering on rooftops
Frost on windshields, Frost chilling your fingers
As you start your morning warming up car,
Preparing yourself to enter workday.
Slight gut tightening, squirming, anticipating
Challenges on the job, facing office
Politics, facing being out maneuvered by
Devious peer freezing you out of power.
Yet while this fearful decline ensues,
Another force arises granting calm
Ability to foil rival's tense
Foretaste of pyrrhic victory over death.
Brief triumph over forces sucking us
Down in miasmic mired decay

●

Death lurking in dried-up grasses, dying
Houseflies, dying beetles, dying rodents
Unable to escape reptile capture
Dying snake caught in woodpile's frozen air.
Death claiming its annual harvest.
Death riding down infirm and unaware.
Death claiming our attachments, our comfort.

Death looking us in the eye and marking time.
Can one die to weak attachments and still
Live in this world – dying to what grips us
What imprisons inner being from it's
Birthright to assume this burden lightly
That continuous worries, dreams, tensions
No longer choke our quiet becoming.

•

As new fires are kindled in woodstove,
Fireplaces and families gather round
A mother suckles her first born child
Her husband planning his son's bright future.

•

Desolate, dark November drawing us
Into our homes to kindle warmth against
Cold air capturing the natural world.
Families gather renewed by closeness.
At first children's rivalry gives way to
Anger igniting father's pent-up anger,
But then a new discovery of warmth
Gathers within his solar plexus as
Something becomes understood about how
To behave as if aligned with inner
Reception of sensed representatives
Welcomed from lighter, finer influences
And we simply know how to be in this
Moment united sensing sacredness.

•

New born child sleeps quietly while
His father and mother each silently
Suffering pressures, responsibilities
Of how to raise this child in this world.

Dying from catastrophic self-contentedness
Each day receiving shocks: is my job safe?
News of child-molester down the street,
Crack-cocaine vials found in the park
Somehow, as fears pile up, a sense of
Ability to sustain one's life by
Simply living with our suffering. Not
Fighting it or wishing it away, just
Being myself receiving anguish and
Loss as what reminds us we're alive.

•

Within each, a new stillness is born
Inviting Sun's silent affirmation.

Mist

As sunlight filters through tree branches,
Mist discretely formed above
Lake surface - gathered in ill-defined restless clumps –
Float just above patient waters as if
Awaiting their opportunity to
Return to their invisible source.
From just above tree tops, Sun penetrates
Air slowly warming, becoming receptive
While one single mist bundle begins
To stretch upward, lifting softly into air
Then slowly disappearing as its essence
Is reabsorbed into atmosphere.
Reclaimed by a source that brought it into
Existence, then resurrection.